Young
Thomas Edison

Great Inventor

A Troll First-Start® Biography

by Claire Nemes
illustrated by John Himmelman

Troll Associates

Library of Congress Cataloging-in-Publication Data

Nemes, Claire.
    Young Thomas Edison: great inventor / by Claire Nemes; illustrated
by John Himmelman.
        p.   cm.— (A Troll first-start biography)
    Summary: A simple biography of the famous American who created
more than 1,000 inventions and became known as "The Wizard of Menlo
Park."
    ISBN 0-8167-3776-2 (lib. bdg.)   ISBN 0-8167-3777-0 (pbk.)
    1. Edison, Thomas A. (Thomas Alva), 1847-1931—Juvenile
literature.   2. Inventors—United States—Biography—Juvenile
literature.   [1. Edison, Thomas A. (Thomas Alva), 1847-1931.
2. Inventors.]   I. Himmelman, John, ill.   II. Title.   III. Series.
TK140.E3N37   1996
621.3'092—dc20
  [B]   95-8107

Thomas Edison was a great inventor. He
made new machines that helped people.
He invented the first electric light, the first
phonograph, and many other things.

Thomas was born in Milan, Ohio, on
February 11, 1847. His parents came to
Ohio from Canada. Thomas was their
youngest son. His full name was Thomas
Alva Edison, but his parents called him "Al."

Milan was a small town, but visitors came all the time. Some were farmers. Sometimes, wagon trains would stop in Milan on their way out West. Al loved talking to the people passing through. He learned from them.

When Al was 7 years old, his family moved
to Michigan. Al started going to school
there. But school was boring!

Al always wanted to learn *more*,
so he asked a lot of questions. So
many questions sometimes made
the teacher angry.

Al left school after only 3 months.
His mother gave him lessons at home.
Al wanted to know about *everything*.
Sometimes, his mother did not have
the answers.

He found many of the answers in books.
But books did not have *all* the answers.
So Al began to experiment and try things
for himself.

When Al was not studying, he was
working. For 3 summers, Al sold fruits
and vegetables with a friend. One summer,
he earned $600. That was a lot of money
in those days!

When he was only 12 years old, Al began to work as a "train boy" for the railway. He sold newspapers and candy on the train.

Al even printed his own newspaper on the train.

He also set up a laboratory there—a place
to try scientific tests or experiments.

But one day, while he was trying an
experiment, he almost set the whole train
on fire!

His boss got very angry. After that, Al had
to sell newspapers at railway stations—
not on the trains.

While he worked for the railway, Al learned how to use the telegraph. This machine allowed people to send messages to faraway places.

From the time he was a boy, Al had
problems with his hearing. But he did not
need to hear well to use the telegraph.
The messages were printed in Morse
code on strips of paper. Al had no trouble
reading the code.

Al decided to become a telegrapher.
He sent and read messages from all over.
His job took him to the South, Canada,
and New England.

The telegraph became more and more
popular. Al wanted to find ways to make
the telegraph work better.

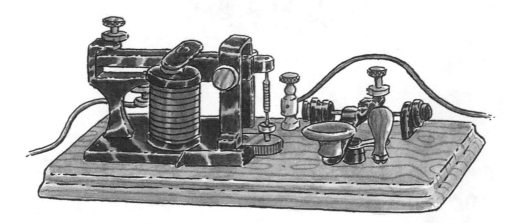

Station One   Station Two

wires

Key (to send)   sounder
                                (to receive)

battery

sounder   Key

message

tape

morse code

A	.−	H	....	O	−−−	V	...−
B	−...	I	..	P	.−−.	W	.−−
C	−.−.	J	.−−−	Q	−−.−	X	−..−
D	−..	K	−.−	R	.−.	Y	−.−−
E	.	L	.−..	S	...	Z	−−..
F	..−.	M	−−	T	−		
G	−−.	N	−.	U	..−		

19

He invented a telegraph that could send 2 messages on the same wire at the same time. And he invented a machine that printed telegraph messages in letters instead of Morse code.

Al decided to make other machines better
and easier to use. He also wanted to make
new machines. He became an inventor.

Al made the typewriter easier to use. He also made the telephone work better.

And he found a way to make motion
pictures that people could watch. He
invented the phonograph, too.

In 1879, Al tried his biggest experiment. He wanted to send electric power to a glass bulb and make it light up. But he needed to put something in the bulb that would glow for a long time. He thought and thought until he found just the right thing.

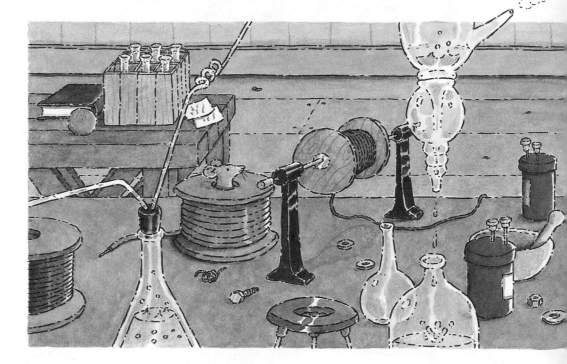

Al put a special metal thread in a bulb and lit it. He looked at it the next day. It was still glowing. Al had invented the electric light! The next step for Al was to open a power station in New York. Now he could bring thousands of lights to the city!

Thomas Edison kept inventing until he died on October 18, 1931. During his life, Edison created more than 1,000 inventions.

He did thousands and thousands of experiments in his lab in Menlo Park, New Jersey. He became very famous. People called him "The Wizard of Menlo Park."

Other inventors might have tried to make things work by using math and drawing plans. They would try to find their answers without experimenting. But not Edison!

Just as he did when he was a boy, Edison loved to find things out for himself. He would try again and again until he made things work.

For one invention, Edison tried about
10,000 experiments. A friend told him not
to feel bad about failing. Edison said,
"Why, I have not failed. I've just found
10,000 ways that won't work."

It's good that he loved to experiment.
Edison made his inventions work because
he never gave up. And the things he
invented have brightened our lives in so
many ways!